W9-BDF-466

THE FRESH KITCHEN

75 Simple Recipes

NUTRI
NINJA

Editors and Content: Meghan Reilly, Kenzie Swanhart, Elizabeth Skladany, and Daniel Davis

Recipe Development: Judy Cannon, Amy Golino, Robyn DeLuca, and Great Flavors Recipe Development Team

Design and Layout: Talia Mangeym

Copywriter: Melissa Stefanini

Creative Director: Lauren Wiernasz

Photo Direction: Lauren Wiernasz and Talia Mangeym

Photography: Michael Piazza and Quentin Bacon

Published in the United States of America by
SharkNinja Operating LLC
180 Wells Avenue
Newton, MA 02459

NN101, NN102 ISBN: 978-1-5323-0625-9

Ninja and Nutri Ninja are registered trademarks of SharkNinja Operating LLC.
Auto-iQ, Auto-iQ Boost, Ninjaccino, Nutri Bowl, and DUO are trademarks of SharkNinja Operating LLC.

10   9   8   7   6   5   4   3   2

Printed in China

NOT ALL FAST FOOD IS CREATED EQUAL.

Meet the Nutri Ninja® Nutri Bowl™ DUO™—it's got all the power and precision you need to get from a.m. to p.m. with fresh, delicious food, fast and easy. Green juice for breakfast? Check. A quick salad for lunch? Done. Whipping up salmon burgers for dinner? Let's do it. There's nothing the Nutri Ninja Nutri Bowl DUO can't handle. Which makes fitting freshness into every part of your life easier than ever before.

TABLE OF CONTENTS

PRODUCT INTRO

NUTRI NINJA® CUP & NUTRI BOWL™

AUTO-iQ BOOST™

FUSION PHILOSOPHY

LOADING INSTRUCTIONS

BUILDING A SMOOTHIE

25

MIDWEST BREAKFAST BURRITOS

34

COFFEE CHIPOTLE CHILE SAUCE

54

62

PRETZEL-COATED CHICKEN FINGERS

93

96

BLUEBERRY LEMON SORBET

120

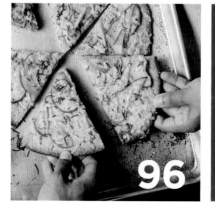

BREAKS INGREDIENTS DOWN.

Your Nutri Ninja® Nutri Bowl™ DUO™ fully breaks down the toughest ingredients—leafy greens, skins, seeds, you name it—leaving no nutrient behind*. If deliciously drinkable juices and smoothies are what you need, the Nutri Ninja cup is the tool you want.

*By blending whole fruits and vegetables, including portions that are usually discarded.

BRINGS INGREDIENTS TOGETHER.

The Nutri Ninja® Nutri Bowl™ DUO™ has all the power and precision you need to make fresh, nutritious snacks, meals and treats, fast and easy. Designed with the perfect ratio of power to size, the Nutri Bowl's Nutrient Fusion* melds ingredients together, turning them into flavorful, complete dishes—which makes fitting freshness into your day easier than ever.

*Create a fusion of foods containing nutrients from fruits, vegetables, and other foods.

CRUISE CONTROL, FOR THE KITCHEN.

Ninja® has set a new standard in drink and meal customization. Auto-iQ Boost™ gives you the power to control the texture and consistency of everything from nutritious juices and smoothies to delectable dips and doughs, all at the touch of a button.

SMOOTHIE

Using frozen fruit? Select **BOOST YES** for the smoothest results. If you're sticking to fresh fruit, you're all set with **BOOST NO**.

TO BOOST OR NOT TO BOOST?

Selecting BOOST YES or BOOST NO adds just the right amount of pulses and pauses to get the results you want from each recipe. Use this guide to get the most out of each program on your Nutri Ninja® Nutri Bowl™ DUO™.

EXTRACT

Select **BOOST YES** if your recipe includes fibrous ingredients with skins and seeds. Otherwise, use **BOOST NO**.

FUSION MIX

Nutri Bowl™ creations are a varied bunch. Choose **BOOST YES** for a smooth consistency; choose **BOOST NO** for a chunkier texture.

FUSION CHOP

Looking for a finer chop of fruits and veggies? Choose **BOOST YES**. Otherwise, choose **BOOST NO**.

FUSION DOUGH

Making dough for pizza or bread? Choose **BOOST YES**. For recipes with extra steps, like pie or cookie dough, choose **BOOST NO**.

GET TO KNOW NUTRIENT FUSION*

Who said meals had to be routine? Nutrient Fusion* transforms diverse, fresh ingredients into flavorful meals and snacks—at the touch of a button. So go ahead, change up that routine and surprise yourself with lively lunches and dinners. Because a good meal shouldn't be a complicated one. And a healthy meal shouldn't be a bland one.

*Create a fusion of foods containing nutrients from fruits, vegetables, and other foods.

SALAD FUSION
Recommended program: Fusion CHOP

Grape & Walnut Chicken Salad
(page 79)

FROZEN FUSION
Recommended program: Fusion MIX

Mango Coconut Ginger Smoothie Bowl
(page 36)

SNACK FUSION
Recommended program: Fusion MIX

Almond Chia Seed Bites
(page 74)

VEGGIE FUSION
Recommended program: Fusion CHOP

Chipotle Salsa
(page 50)

PROTEIN FUSION
Recommended program: Fusion CHOP

Salmon Burgers
(page 77)

WHOLE GRAIN FUSION
Recommended program: Fusion DOUGH

Pear, Gruyère & Rosemary Flatbread
(page 96)

SWEET FUSION
Recommended program: Fusion DOUGH

Salted Caramel Chip Cookies
(page 119)

LOAD IT UP.

It's time to take your Nutri Ninja® Nutri Bowl™ DUO™ for a spin.
When it comes to loading the containers, order is everything. Use these quick tips
and visual guide to ensure your recipes turn out just the way you want them, every time.

Don't overfill the Nutri Ninja® cups.
If you feel resistance when attaching
the Pro Extractor Blades® Assembly
to the cup, remove some ingredients.

When loading the
Nutri Bowl™, make sure
ingredients do not go
past the max fill line.

CAUTION: Remove the Pro Extractor Blades® Assembly from the Nutri Ninja® cup upon completion of blending.
Do not store ingredients before or after blending in the cup with the blade assembly attached. Some foods may contain
active ingredients or release gases that will expand if left in a sealed container, resulting in excessive pressure buildup
that can pose a risk of injury. For ingredient storage, only use Spout Lid to cover.

5 Top off with ice or frozen ingredients.

4 Next add any dry or sticky ingredients like seeds, powders, and nut butters.

3 Pour in liquid or yogurt next.

For thinner results or a juice-like drink, add more liquid as desired.

2 Next add leafy greens and herbs.

START FROM THE BOTTOM UP

1 Start by adding fresh fruits and vegetables.

(Note: For best results, cut ingredients in 1-inch chunks. Do not place frozen ingredients first in the Nutri Ninja® cups).

BUILD THE PERFECT SMOOTHIE.

The perfect smoothie is a sum of its parts. Choose an ingredient from each column for the most delicious results.

CHOOSE YOUR BASE

Almond milk

Coconut milk

Rice milk

Soy milk

Fresh juice

Chilled green tea

Coconut water

Maple water

Water

CHOOSE YOUR FRUIT

Apples

Bananas

Blackberries

Blueberries

Raspberries

Strawberries

Cherries

Kiwis

Mangoes

Oranges

Peaches

Pineapple

MAKE IT GREEN

Kale

Spinach

Watercress

Cabbage

Celery

Cucumber

Fresh mint

MAKE IT THICK & CREAMY

Avocado

Chia seeds

Coconut

Greek yogurt

Ice

Nut butter

Nuts

Oats

KICK IT UP A NOTCH

Bee pollen

Cacao powder

Cinnamon

Coconut oil

Fresh ginger

Flaxseed

Protein powder

Maca powder

Matcha powder

Spirulina

Turmeric

ADD A LITTLE SWEETNESS

Agave nectar

Dates

Figs

Honey

Maple syrup

Vanilla extract

Stevia

APPLE
PIE
SMOOTHIE

Prep time: 5 minutes
Container: 24-ounce Tritan™ Nutri Ninja® Cup
Makes: 4 (8-ounce) servings

INGREDIENTS

1 Golden Delicious apple,
peeled, cored, cut in quarters

1 cup unsweetened almond milk

$3/4$ teaspoon lemon juice

$1\,1/2$ teaspoons brown sugar

$1/4$ teaspoon ground cinnamon

$1/8$ teaspoon ground nutmeg

$1/8$ teaspoon salt

1 cup ice

DIRECTIONS

1. Place all ingredients into the 24-ounce Tritan Nutri Ninja Cup in the order listed.

2. Select Auto-iQ™ BOOST YES SMOOTHIE.

3. Remove blades from cup after blending.

SUNFLOWER PROTEIN PIZZAZZ

Prep time: 5 minutes
Container: 24-ounce Tritan™ Nutri Ninja® Cup
Makes: 1 (14-ounce) serving

INGREDIENTS

1 ripe banana

²/₃ cup almond milk

2 ¹/₂ tablespoons
sunflower butter (page 71)

2 ¹/₂ teaspoons unsweetened
cocoa powder

1 scoop chocolate
protein powder

1 ¹/₃ cups ice

DIRECTIONS

1. Place all ingredients into the 24-ounce Tritan Nutri Ninja Cup in the order listed.

2. Select Auto-iQ™ BOOST YES SMOOTHIE.

3. Remove blades from cup after blending.

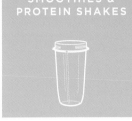

CUCUMBER MELON QUENCH

Prep time: 5 minutes
Container: 24-ounce Tritan™ Nutri Ninja® Cup
Makes: 1 (16-ounce) serving

INGREDIENTS

3-inch piece English cucumber, peeled, cut in 1-inch chunks

1 cup green grapes

1/3 cup honeydew melon chunks

1/2 orange, peeled, seeds removed

1/2 cup baby spinach

1/2 cup water

1/2 cup ice

DIRECTIONS

1. Place all ingredients into the 24-ounce Tritan Nutri Ninja Cup in the order listed.

2. Select Auto-iQ™ BOOST YES EXTRACT.

3. Remove blades from cup after blending.

CRANBERRY
OAT
SOOTHER

Prep time: 5 minutes
Container: 24-ounce Tritan™ Nutri Ninja® Cup
Makes: 2 (10-ounce) servings

INGREDIENTS

½ cup walnut pieces

⅓ cup whole-berry
cranberry sauce

1 cup oat milk

¼ teaspoon vanilla

1 tablespoon honey

¼ teaspoon salt

1 ½ cups ice

DIRECTIONS

1. Place all ingredients into the 24-ounce Tritan Nutri Ninja
   Cup in the order listed.

2. Select Auto-iQ™ BOOST YES EXTRACT.

3. Remove blades from cup after blending.

PREP SUGGESTION

Freeze fresh berries when they are perfectly ripe to enjoy a taste of summer long after the picking season.

ORANGE
BLUSH

Prep time: 5 minutes
Container: 24-ounce Tritan™ Nutri Ninja® Cup
Makes: 2 (10-ounce) servings

INGREDIENTS

½ cup watermelon chunks

¾ cup orange juice

1 cup frozen strawberries

½ cup ice

DIRECTIONS

1. Place all ingredients into the 24-ounce Tritan Nutri Ninja Cup in the order listed.

2. Select Auto-iQ™ BOOST YES SMOOTHIE.

3. Remove blades from cup after blending.

STRAWBERRY BANANA PROTEIN SHAKE

Prep time: 5 minutes
Container: 24-ounce Tritan™ Nutri Ninja® Cup
Makes: 2 (8-ounce) servings

INGREDIENTS

1 small ripe banana

$1/3$ cup nonfat Greek yogurt

$3/4$ cup orange juice

2 scoops protein powder

$3/4$ cup frozen strawberries

DIRECTIONS

1. Place all ingredients into the 24-ounce Tritan Nutri Ninja Cup in the order listed.

2. Select Auto-iQ™ BOOST NO SMOOTHIE.

3. Remove blades from cup after blending.

MANGO PROTEIN SHAKE

Prep time: 2 minutes
Container: 24-ounce Tritan™ Nutri Ninja™ Cup
Makes: 2 (10-ounce) servings

INGREDIENTS

2 cups 1% milk

2 scoops vanilla protein powder

¼ cup frozen mango chunks

DIRECTIONS

1. Place all ingredients into the 24-ounce Tritan Nutri Ninja Cup in the order listed.

2. Select Auto-iQ™ BOOST NO SMOOTHIE.

2. Remove blades from cup after blending.

MOCHA NINJACCINO™

Prep time: 5 minutes
Container: 24-ounce Tritan™ Nutri Ninja® Cup
Makes: 2 (8-ounce) servings

INGREDIENTS

1/2 cup plus 1 tablespoon double-strength brewed coffee, chilled

3 cups ice

1/4 cup 1% milk

1/4 cup chocolate syrup, plus more for garnish

Whipped cream, for garnish

DIRECTIONS

1. Place all ingredients, except whipped cream, into the 24-ounce Tritan Nutri Ninja Cup in the order listed.

2. Select Auto-iQ™ BOOST YES SMOOTHIE.

3. Remove blades from cup after blending.

4. Divide between 2 glasses, top with whipped cream, and drizzle with chocolate syrup.

DO NOT BLEND HOT INGREDIENTS.

MORNING BERRY

Prep time: 5 minutes
Container: 24-ounce Tritan™ Nutri Ninja® Cup
Makes: 2 (10-ounce) servings

INGREDIENTS

1 medium ripe banana

1 $1/2$ cups almond milk

3 tablespoons honey

2 tablespoons flaxseed

1 $1/2$ cups frozen mixed berries

DIRECTIONS

1. Place all ingredients into the 24-ounce Tritan Nutri Ninja Cup in the order listed.

2. Select Auto-iQ™ BOOST YES EXTRACT.

3. Remove blades from cup after blending.

CHOCOLATE PEANUT BUTTER PROTEIN SHAKE

Prep time: 2 minutes
Container: 24-ounce Tritan™ Nutri Ninja™ Cup
Makes: 2 (10-ounce) servings

INGREDIENTS

³/₄ cup kale, stems removed

1 ½ cups unsweetened coconut milk

1 scoop chocolate protein powder

2 tablespoons peanut butter

1 medium frozen ripe banana

³/₄ cup ice

DIRECTIONS

1. Place all ingredients into the 24-ounce Tritan Nutri Ninja Cup in the order listed.

2. Select Auto-iQ™ BOOST YES SMOOTHIE.

3. Remove blades from cup after blending.

PECAN PRALINE NINJACCINO™

Prep time: 5 minutes
Container: 24-ounce Tritan™ Nutri Ninja® Cup
Makes: 2 (10-ounce) servings

INGREDIENTS

½ cup plus 1 tablespoon double-strength brewed coffee, chilled

¼ cup toasted pecans

¼ cup 1% milk

2 tablespoons butterscotch or caramel sauce

2 tablespoons packed dark brown sugar

¼ teaspoon vanilla extract

3 cups ice

DIRECTIONS

1. Place all ingredients into the 24-ounce Tritan Nutri Ninja Cup in the order listed.

2. Select Auto-iQ™ BOOST YES SMOOTHIE.

3. Remove blades from cup after blending.

DO NOT BLEND HOT INGREDIENTS.

MIDWEST BREAKFAST BURRITOS

Prep time: 10 minutes   **Cook time:** 5 minutes
Container: Nutri Bowl™
Makes: 6 servings

INGREDIENTS

¼ cup (4 ounces) ham,
cut in 2-inch cubes

½ medium green bell pepper,
cut in quarters, seeds removed

½ cup low-fat cheddar cheese,
cubed

¼ small onion, cut in half

9 large eggs

¼ teaspoon salt

½ teaspoon ground black pepper

6 (6-inch) whole wheat tortillas,
for serving

1 ½ cups salsa, for serving

DIRECTIONS

1. Place all ingredients, except tortillas and salsa, into the Nutri Bowl in the order listed.

2. Select Auto-iQ™ BOOST YES Fusion CHOP.

3. Lightly spray a skillet with cooking spray and place over medium-high heat. Add egg mixture and stir until eggs are cooked through.

4. Divide egg mixture between the tortillas and top with salsa. Roll up each tortilla and serve.

COCONUT LIME BARS

Prep time: 10 minutes **Chill time:** 2 hours
Container: Nutri Bowl™
Makes: 16 servings

INGREDIENTS

1 cup dried apricots

2 cups toasted macadamia nuts

1/4 cup pumpkin seeds

2 tablespoons hemp seed

1/2 cup unsweetened shredded coconut

1 teaspoon lime zest

1 teaspoon lime juice

1 tablespoon agave nectar

2 tablespoons water

1/8 teaspoon salt

DIRECTIONS

1. Line an 8x8-inch baking dish with plastic wrap; set aside.

2. Place all ingredients into the Nutri Bowl in the order listed. Select Auto-iQ™ BOOST YES Fusion MIX.

3. Firmly press mixture into the prepared baking dish and evenly disperse. Chill for at least 2 hours before cutting into 16 pieces. Store in the refrigerator, covered, up to 1 week.

DO NOT BLEND HOT INGREDIENTS.

MANGO COCONUT GINGER SMOOTHIE BOWL

Prep time: 5 minutes
Container: Nutri Bowl™
Makes: 2 cups

INGREDIENTS

SMOOTHIE

1 ½ cups frozen mango chunks

1 tablespoon lime juice

¼-inch piece fresh ginger, peeled

¾ cup coconut milk

TOPPINGS

Shredded coconut

Macadamia nuts

Fresh pineapple chunks

Fresh blueberries

Granola

DIRECTIONS

1. Place all smoothie ingredients into the Nutri Bowl in the order listed.

2. Select Auto-iQ™ BOOST YES Fusion MIX.

3. Place in bowl and add toppings.

RED VELVET PANCAKES

Prep time: 5 minutes **Cook time:** 10 minutes
Container: Nutri Bowl™
Makes: 6 pancakes

INGREDIENTS

½ cup buttermilk

2 teaspoons vanilla extract

1 cup pancake mix

1 tablespoon unsweetened cocoa powder

1 tablespoons sugar

1 large egg, lightly beaten

DIRECTIONS

1. Position the Dough Blade Assembly in the Nutri Bowl, then add all ingredients in the order listed.

2. Select Auto-iQ™ BOOST YES Fusion DOUGH.

3. Heat an 8-inch skillet over medium heat and lightly coat with nonstick cooking spray.

4. Pour ¼ cup of batter into the skillet. Cook until bubbles form on top, about 1 ½ minutes, then flip and cook for 1 minute. Repeat process with the rest of the batter. Serve immediately.

PEANUT BUTTER PROTEIN BARS

Prep time: 10 minutes **Cook time:** 10 minutes **Cool time:** 1 hour
Container: Nutri Bowl™
Makes: 14 (2-ounce) servings

INGREDIENTS

1 cup unsalted peanuts

2 ¹/₂ cups old-fashioned rolled oats

³/₄ cup milk

1 cup peanut butter

¹/₄ cup honey

1 scoop vanilla protein powder

DIRECTIONS

1. Preheat oven to 350°F. Line a baking pan with parchment paper; set aside.

2. Place peanuts into the Nutri Bowl. Select Auto-iQ™ BOOST YES Fusion CHOP.

3. Place peanuts and oats on prepared baking pan and cook until golden brown, about 10 minutes.

4. Add milk, peanut butter, and honey to saucepan over medium-low heat, stirring until warmed. Add peanut/oat mixture and protein powder. Cook for 1 minute.

5. Line a 13x9-inch baking pan with parchment paper. Pour mixture into pan, spreading evenly. Place a sheet of plastic wrap on top and press firmly. Cool for 1 hour before serving.

SERVING SUGGESTION

Serve with your favorite blueberry jam or preserves.

LEMON GINGER SCONES

Prep time: 15 minutes **Cook time:** 18 minutes **Rest time:** 15 minutes
Container: Nutri Bowl™
Makes: 8 scones

INGREDIENTS

DOUGH

1 cup all-purpose flour

$1/8$ teaspoon salt

2 tablespoons sugar

2 teaspoons baking powder

Zest of $1/2$ lemon

1 teaspoon crystallized ginger, finely minced

2 tablespoons cold unsalted butter, cut in $1/2$-inch cubes

$1/3$ cup plus 1 tablespoon milk

ICING

1 cup confectioners' sugar

2 tablespoons fresh lemon juice

1 teaspoon crystallized ginger, finely minced

DIRECTIONS

1. Preheat oven to 375°F. Line a baking sheet with parchment paper; set aside.

2. In a medium bowl, whisk together flour, salt, sugar, baking powder, lemon zest, and 1 teaspoon crystallized ginger.

3. Position the Dough Blade Assembly in the Nutri Bowl, then add the dry-ingredient mixture, butter, and milk.

4. Select Auto-iQ™ BOOST YES Fusion CHOP. Mixture should not be fully incorporated.

5. Place dough onto a lightly floured surface and gently knead to form a 1-inch thick circle. Cut dough into 8 triangles. Place triangles onto prepared baking sheet and bake for 18 minutes, or until light golden brown.

6. To make the icing, whisk together confectioners' sugar, lemon juice, and 1 teaspoon crystallized ginger until smooth.

7. Coat scones with icing and let sit for 15 minutes or until icing is slightly hardened.

SPINACH & CHEDDAR EGG MUFFINS

Prep time: 10 minutes **Cook time:** 23–25 minutes
Container: Nutri Bowl™
Makes: 12 egg cups (6 servings)

INGREDIENTS

³/₄ cup baby spinach

¹/₂ cup aged cheddar cheese

¹/₂ red bell pepper,
seeds removed, chopped

¹/₄ medium onion

5 cherry tomatoes

7 large eggs

¹/₂ cup milk

³/₄ teaspoon salt

³/₄ teaspoon ground
black pepper

DIRECTIONS

1. Preheat oven to 350°F. Lightly coat a 12-cup nonstick muffin pan with cooking spray.

2. Place spinach, cheese, red pepper, onion, and tomatoes into the Nutri Bowl. Select Auto-iQ™ BOOST YES Fusion CHOP.

3. In a medium mixing bowl, whisk the chopped mixture with eggs, milk, salt, and pepper. Evenly divide mixture between muffin cups. Bake until knife inserted in center comes out clean, about 23 to 25 minutes.

FRENCH ONION TOFU DIP

Prep time: 25 minutes **Cook time:** 7–9 minutes
Container: 24-ounce Tritan™ Nutri Ninja® Cup
Makes: 1 ½ cups

INGREDIENTS

1 tablespoon vegetable oil

1 medium yellow onion, chopped

½ teaspoon salt

¼ teaspoon ground black pepper

3 tablespoons malt vinegar

½ cup firm tofu

½ package (4 ounces) non-fat cream cheese, softened

⅓ cup nonfat sour cream

DIRECTIONS

1. In a 10-inch sauté pan over medium heat, add the oil, onion, salt, and pepper. Cook 6 to 8 minutes, stirring occasionally, until caramelized. Add the malt vinegar and cook for 1 minute.

2. Remove from heat and let cool.

3. Place the cooled onion mixture, tofu, cream cheese, and sour cream into the 24-ounce Tritan Nutri Ninja Cup.

4. Select START/STOP and blend to desired texture. Remove blades from cup after blending.

DO NOT BLEND HOT INGREDIENTS.

CLASSIC HUMMUS

Prep time: 5 minutes
Container: Nutri Bowl™
Makes: 2 ½ cups

INGREDIENTS

2 cups cooked, drained garbanzo beans (liquid reserved)

¼ cup plus 2 tablespoons garbanzo bean liquid

¼ cup lemon juice

¼ cup olive oil

1 clove garlic, peeled

2 tablespoons tahini

1 teaspoon ground cumin

DIRECTIONS

1. Place all ingredients into the Nutri Bowl in the order listed.

2. Select Auto-iQ™ BOOST YES Fusion MIX.

SPINACH ARTICHOKE DIP

Prep time: 10 minutes **Cook time:** 20 minutes
Container: Nutri Bowl™
Makes: 4 cups

INGREDIENTS

¼ cup mayonnaise

¼ cup sour cream

1 package (8 ounces)
cream cheese

2 tablespoons lemon juice

½ cup shredded lowfat
mozzarella cheese

¼ cup grated Parmesan cheese

4 cloves garlic, peeled

1 can (14 ounces) artichoke
hearts, drained

1 cup frozen spinach, thawed,
squeezed of excess liquid

DIRECTIONS

1. Preheat oven to 350°F.

2. Place all ingredients, except the artichoke and spinach, into the Nutri Bowl. Select Auto-iQ™ BOOST NO Fusion MIX.

3. Add artichoke and spinach to the bowl and Select Auto-iQ BOOST NO Fusion CHOP.

4. Carefully remove the blades and spoon the dip into a heat-resistant baking dish. Bake for 20 minutes, or until golden brown and bubbly. Serve warm with pita chips or sliced French bread.

DO NOT BLEND HOT INGREDIENTS.

BABA GHANOUSH

Prep time: 8 minutes **Cook time:** 15 minutes
Container: Nutri Bowl™
Makes: 4–6 servings

INGREDIENTS

1 large eggplant

1/2 teaspoon plus 2 tablespoons olive oil, divided

1/4 medium onion

2 cloves garlic, peeled

2 tablespoons lemon juice

2 tablespoons tahini

1/4 teaspoon smoked paprika

1/2 teaspoon salt

1/4 teaspoon ground black pepper

DIRECTIONS

1. Preheat oven to 450°F. Lightly coat a baking pan with cooking spray.

2. Cut eggplant in half and rub with 1/2 teaspoon olive oil. Place cut side down on baking pan and cook until skin is charred and interior is tender, 20 to 30 minutes. Let cool and then scoop out flesh.

3. Place the cooled eggplant, 2 tablespoons olive oil, and remaining ingredients into the Nutri Bowl.

4. Select Auto-iQ™ BOOST YES Fusion MIX.

DO NOT BLEND HOT INGREDIENTS.

GARLIC & HERB AIOLI

Prep time: 5 minutes
Container: Nutri Bowl™
Makes: 1 cup

INGREDIENTS

4 egg yolks*

½ cup fresh basil leaves

2 cloves garlic, peeled

1 tablespoon water

1 tablespoon lemon juice

1 teaspoon Dijon mustard

¼ teaspoon salt

¼ teaspoon ground white pepper

1 cup canola oil

Warning: This recipe contains raw eggs.

DIRECTIONS

1. Place all ingredients, except oil, into the Nutri Bowl in the order listed.

2. Select Auto-iQ™ BOOST YES Fusion MIX and slowly drizzle in oil until fully incorporated.

CHIPOTLE SALSA

Prep time: 5 minutes
Container: Nutri Bowl™
Makes: 4 cups

INGREDIENTS

1 can (14 ounces) whole peeled tomatoes

1 white onion, cut in quarters

¼ cup cilantro leaves

1 jalapeño pepper, seeds removed

1 chipotle pepper in adobo sauce

2 tablespoons adobo sauce

1 lime, peeled, cut in quarters, seeds removed

Salt and pepper, to taste

DIRECTIONS

1. Place all ingredients into the Nutri Bowl in the order listed.

2. Select Auto-iQ™ BOOST NO Fusion CHOP.

INGREDIENT SUGGESTION

For a salsa verde, substitute fresh or canned tomatillos for the tomatoes.

RECIPE SUGGESTION

Swap out the basil for arugula to give this pesto a peppery flavor.

BASIL PESTO

Prep time: 5 minutes
Container: Nutri Bowl™
Makes: 4–6 servings

INGREDIENTS

¼ cup toasted pine nuts

2 large cloves garlic, peeled

1 ½ cups fresh basil

¼ cup grated Parmesan cheese

¼ teaspoon salt

¼ teaspoon ground black pepper

⅓ cup extra-virgin olive oil

DIRECTIONS

1. Place all ingredients into the Nutri Bowl in the order listed.

2. Select Auto-iQ™ BOOST YES Fusion MIX.

DO NOT BLEND HOT INGREDIENTS.

COFFEE CHIPOTLE CHILE SAUCE

Prep time: 5 minutes
Container: 24-ounce Tritan™ Nutri Ninja® Cup
Makes: 2 cups

INGREDIENTS

1 cup ketchup

1/2 cup strongly brewed coffee, cooled

1/4 cup apple cider vinegar

1/4 cup cilantro

1/4 cup light brown sugar

1 tablespoon chipotle peppers in adobo sauce

1 tablespoon Dijon mustard

1 tablespoon instant coffee granules

1/8 teaspoon ground cloves

DIRECTIONS

1. Place all ingredients into the 24-ounce Tritan Nutri Ninja Cup in the order listed.

2. Select START/STOP for 20 seconds.

3. Remove blades from cup after blending.

DO NOT BLEND HOT INGREDIENTS.

NO-COOK HOLLANDAISE SAUCE

Prep time: 5 minutes
Container: Nutri Bowl™
Makes: 1/2 cup

INGREDIENTS

2 egg yolks*

1 tablespoon lemon juice

1/2 teaspoon salt

1/8 teaspoon cayenne pepper

1 stick (4 ounces) unsalted butter, melted

Warning: This recipe contains raw eggs.

DIRECTIONS

1. Place egg yolks, lemon juice, salt, and cayenne pepper into the Nutri Bowl.

2. Select Auto-iQ™ BOOST YES Fusion MIX and slowly drizzle in melted butter until fully incorporated, about 60 seconds.

CASHEW ALFREDO SAUCE

Prep time: 5 minutes **Soak time:** 2 hours
Container: Nutri Bowl™
Makes: 8 (¼-cup) servings

INGREDIENTS

1 ½ cups cashews

1 ½ cups almond milk

½ cup nutritional yeast

3 cloves garlic, peeled

½ teaspoon salt

½ teaspoon ground white pepper

DIRECTIONS

1. Place cashews in a bowl. Cover with water and let soak for 2 hours. Drain well.

2. Place all ingredients into the Nutri Bowl in the order listed.

3. Select Auto-iQ™ BOOST YES Fusion MIX.

SERVING SUGGESTION

Serve atop your favorite pasta or vegetable noodles.

ROSEMARY MUSTARD MARINADE

Prep time: 5 minutes
Container: 24-ounce Tritan™ Nutri Ninja® Cup
Makes: 1 cup

INGREDIENTS

2 lemons, peeled, cut in half, seeds removed

$\frac{1}{2}$ cup olive oil

$\frac{1}{4}$ cup whole-grain mustard

3 tablespoons fresh rosemary, chopped

2 cloves garlic, peeled

1 teaspoon salt

1 teaspoon ground black pepper

DIRECTIONS

1. Place all ingredients into the 24-ounce Tritan Nutri Ninja Cup in the order listed.

2. Select START/STOP for 20 seconds.

3. Remove blades from cup after blending.

SHRIMP
& BACON STUFFED
MUSHROOMS

Prep time: 10 minutes **Cook time**: 20 minutes
Container: Nutri Bowl™
Makes: 6–8 servings

INGREDIENTS

1 tablespoon canola oil

5 slices uncooked bacon, chopped

1/2 medium onion, chopped

3 cloves garlic, peeled, chopped

1/2 pound uncooked medium shrimp, peeled, deveined

3/4 cup shredded white cheddar cheese

1/2 cup bread crumbs

1/4 cup mayonnaise

1 tablespoon horseradish

24 baby bella mushrooms, stems removed

DIRECTIONS

1. Preheat oven to 350°F. Line a baking pan with parchment paper.

2. Heat oil in a medium sauté pan over medium-high heat. Sauté bacon until almost fully cooked. Add onion, garlic, and shrimp. Cook 2 to 3 minutes, or until onions are softened. Cool mixture.

3. Place shrimp mixture into the Nutri Bowl. Select Auto-iQ™ BOOST YES Fusion CHOP.

4. Transfer mixture to a medium mixing bowl. Add cheese, bread crumbs, mayonnaise, and horseradish. Stir to combine.

5. Place shrimp filling into mushrooms. Place mushrooms on prepared pan and bake 20 minutes, or until mushrooms are soft and filling begins to brown.

DO NOT BLEND HOT INGREDIENTS.

CHILI LIME SWEET POTATO BOWL

Prep time: 10 minutes
Container: Nutri Bowl™
Makes: 2 servings

INGREDIENTS

BOWL

1 medium cooked sweet potato, peeled, cooled

½ cup canned white beans, drained

2 tablespoons lime juice

1 tablespoon coconut oil, melted

½ teaspoon cumin

TOPPINGS

Roasted corn

Sliced red pepper

Pepitas

Cilantro

Chili powder

Cotija cheese

Avocado

DIRECTIONS

1. Place all ingredients, except those for toppings, into the Nutri Bowl in the order listed.

2. Select Auto-iQ™ BOOST YES Fusion MIX.

3. Add desired toppings.

DO NOT BLEND HOT INGREDIENTS.

CREAMLESS CAULIFLOWER & CHICKEN SOUP

Prep time: 5 minutes **Cook time:** 10 minutes **Cool time:** 20 minutes
Container: 24-ounce Tritan™ Nutri Ninja® Cup
Makes: 4 (6-ounce) servings

INGREDIENTS

3 cups cauliflower

3 cups low-sodium chicken broth

1 medium carrot, peeled,
cut in 1-inch pieces

$1/2$-inch piece fresh ginger, peeled

$1/2$ teaspoon paprika

$1/2$ teaspoon salt

$1/4$ teaspoon ground black pepper

$1 1/2$ cups cooked chicken,
diced, warm

DIRECTIONS

1. Place all ingredients, except chicken, into a medium saucepan. Cook over medium-high heat until cauliflower and carrots are tender, about 10 minutes. Allow mixture to cool, about 20 minutes.

2. Place cooled mixture into the 24-ounce Tritan Nutri Ninja Cup.

3. Select START/STOP for 30 seconds.

4. Remove blades from cup after blending.

5. Reheat soup in a saucepan. Place cooked chicken in each bowl and pour hot soup on top.

DO NOT BLEND HOT INGREDIENTS.

TUNA TARTARE

Prep time: 5 minutes
Container: Nutri Bowl™
Makes: 1 cup

INGREDIENTS

½ pound fresh sushi-grade tuna*

2 tablespoons green onions, chopped

1 tablespoon soy sauce

1 teaspoon lime juice

1 teaspoon sesame seeds

1 teaspoon wasabi powder

¾ teaspoon olive oil

½ teaspoon fresh minced ginger

Warning: This recipe contains uncooked fish.

DIRECTIONS

1. Place all ingredients into the Nutri Bowl in the order listed.

2. Select Auto-iQ™ BOOST YES Fusion CHOP.

**SERVING
SUGGESTION**

Serve with Flax &
Sesame Seed Crackers
(page 65).

FLAX & SESAME SEED CRACKERS

Prep time: 10 minutes **Rest time:** 15 minutes **Cook time:** 1 hour 40 minutes
Container: Nutri Bowl™
Makes: 26 crackers

INGREDIENTS

1 cup water

½ cup flaxseeds

⅓ cup sesame seeds

¼ cup chia seeds

½ teaspoon salt

½ teaspoon ground black pepper

½ teaspoon ground coriander

½ teaspoon onion powder

DIRECTIONS

1. Preheat oven to 375°F. Line a baking sheet with aluminum foil and lightly coat with cooking spray; set aside.

2. Place all ingredients into a mixing bowl. Let rest for 15 minutes.

3. Position the Dough Blade Assembly in the Nutri Bowl, then add all ingredients in the order listed. Select Auto-iQ™ BOOST YES Fusion DOUGH.

4. Spoon batter onto the prepared baking sheet and smooth it out to form a very thin layer without holes. Bake 40 minutes.

5. With a pizza cutter, cut crackers into desired shape. Place baking sheet back into the oven and bake for another 1 hour, or until crackers are very crispy.

6. Let crackers cool completely before serving.

SHRIMP TOAST

Prep time: 10 minutes **Cook time:** 8 minutes
Container: Nutri Bowl™
Makes: 6 servings

INGREDIENTS

½ pound uncooked medium
shrimp, peeled, deveined

1-inch piece fresh ginger, peeled

2 cloves garlic, peeled

2 green onions,
cut in 1-inch pieces

1 large egg white

1 tablespoon sesame oil

1 tablespoon soy sauce

6 slices thick-cut white bread

2 cups canola oil, for frying

DIRECTIONS

1. Place all ingredients, except bread and canola oil, into the Nutri Bowl. Select START/STOP for 15 seconds.

2. Spread shrimp mixture on each slice of bread, divided evenly.

3. Add oil to a large sauté pan over medium-high heat. Once oil is hot, carefully add a slice of bread with shrimp side down. Cook 2 minutes per side, or until golden brown. Carefully remove from pan and cut into 4 triangles. Repeat with remaining bread slices.

AVOCADO TOAST

Prep time: 8 minutes **Cook time:** 5 minutes
Container: Nutri Bowl™
Makes: 4 servings

INGREDIENTS

1 ripe avocado,
pit removed, peeled

1 tablespoon sriracha sauce

4 slices whole-wheat bread,
toasted

4 slices cooked turkey bacon,
chopped

DIRECTIONS

1. Place avocado and sriracha into the Nutri Bowl.

2. Select Auto-iQ™ BOOST NO Fusion CHOP.

3. Top each slice of toasted bread with pureed avocado and chopped turkey bacon.

HERBED CRACKERS

Prep time: 8 minutes **Cook time:** 14 minutes
Container: Nutri Bowl™
Makes: 16 servings

INGREDIENTS

1 cup all-purpose flour

½ teaspoon salt

½ teaspoon ground black pepper

1 teaspoon Italian seasoning

2 tablespoons cold unsalted butter, cut in ½-inch pieces

⅓ cup water

DIRECTIONS

1. Preheat oven to 400°F.

2. Place all ingredients into the Nutri Bowl. Select Auto-iQ™ BOOST NO Fusion DOUGH.

3. Place dough onto a lightly floured surface and roll into a rectangle ⅛-inch thick. Place the rolled dough onto an ungreased baking sheet. Prick dough with a fork and cut into desired cracker shapes.

4. Bake 14 minutes or until light golden brown. Let cool completely before serving.

SERVING SUGGESTION

This seed butter is great for those with peanut allergies—use it on sandwiches or in your favorite cookie recipes.

SUNFLOWER BUTTER

Prep time: 5 minutes
Container: Nutri Bowl™
Makes: 1 ¼ cups

INGREDIENTS

2 cups roasted unsalted sunflower seeds

3 tablespoons coconut oil, melted

1 tablespoon honey

¼ teaspoon salt

DIRECTIONS

1. Place sunflower seeds into the Nutri Bowl, then select START/STOP for 30 seconds or until finely ground.

2. Add oil and select START/STOP for 60 seconds. Scrape down sides of bowl. Select START/STOP for another 60 seconds, or until smooth.

3. Add honey and salt to the Nutri Bowl, then select START/STOP for 60 seconds.

PARMESAN TRUFFLE POPCORN

Prep time: 5 minutes
Container: Nutri Bowl™
Makes: 4 servings

INGREDIENTS

¼ cup (2 ounces) Parmesan cheese, cut in 1-inch pieces

1 tablespoon plus 1 teaspoon black truffle oil

1 bag (3.25 ounces) natural plain microwave popcorn

DIRECTIONS

1. Place Parmesan cheese into the Nutri Bowl. Select START/STOP for 45 seconds.

2. Cook popcorn according to package directions. Once popped, transfer to a large bowl.

3. Sprinkle with Parmesan cheese and truffle oil and toss until combined.

STRAWBERRY FRUIT LEATHER

Prep time: 5 minutes **Cook time:** 3 hours **Set time:** 12 hours
Container: Nutri Bowl™
Makes: 8 servings

INGREDIENTS

2 cups strawberries,
hulled, cut in half

3 tablespoons sugar

2 teaspoons lemon juice

DIRECTIONS

1. Preheat oven to 175°F. Line a baking pan with a silicone baking mat or parchment paper; set aside.

2. Place all ingredients into the Nutri Bowl. Select START/STOP for 45 seconds. Pour mixture into prepared pan and evenly spread in a thin layer.

3. Bake 3 hours or until mixture is set and dry to the touch. Remove from oven and let sit, uncovered, for 12 hours. Carefully remove from pan and cut into 1 ½-inch strips.

ALMOND CHIA SEED BITES

Prep time: 15 minutes **Chill time:** 1 hour
Container: Nutri Bowl™
Makes: 24 bites (6 servings)

INGREDIENTS

½ cup almonds

½ cup dark chocolate chips

6 dates, cut in half, pits removed

1 tablespoon coconut oil, melted

½ cup almond butter

1 tablespoon chia seed

1 cup old-fashioned rolled oats

DIRECTIONS

1. Place all ingredients, except oats, into the Nutri Bowl in the order listed. Select Auto-iQ™ BOOST YES Fusion MIX.

2. Add rolled oats and PULSE to combine.

3. Roll dough into 24 evenly sized bites, about 1 ¼ inches round. Refrigerate for 1 hour before serving.

BROWN RICE SESAME PANCAKES

Prep time: 15 minutes **Cook time:** 20 minutes
Container: Nutri Bowl™
Makes: 12 pancakes (6 servings)

INGREDIENTS

2 large eggs

³/₄ cup cooked brown rice, cooled

2 tablespoons sesame seeds

1 tablespoons ground flaxseed

¹/₄ teaspoon baking powder

¹/₄ teaspoon salt

DIRECTIONS

1. Place all ingredients into the Nutri Bowl in the order listed.

2. Select Auto-iQ™ BOOST YES Fusion CHOP.

3. Heat a medium nonstick sauté pan over medium heat. Pour 1 tablespoon batter onto the pan. Cook batter for 2 minutes, then flip and cook an additional 2 minutes. Repeat with remaining batter.

DO NOT BLEND HOT INGREDIENTS.

SALMON BURGERS

Prep time: 10 minutes **Cook time:** 6 minutes
Container: Nutri Bowl™
Makes: 4 servings

INGREDIENTS

2 green onions,
cut in 2-inch pieces

1 ¼ pounds uncooked
boneless, skinless salmon,
cut in 2-inch chunks

2 teaspoons Dijon mustard

1 tablespoon lemon juice

1 large egg

¾ teaspoon crab seasoning

½ teaspoon ground black pepper

¼ cup panko bread crumbs

DIRECTIONS

1. Place all ingredients into the Nutri Bowl in the order listed.

2. Select Auto-iQ™ BOOST YES Fusion CHOP. Form mixture into 4 burgers.

3. Spray a nonstick skillet or grill pan with vegetable cooking spray over medium-high heat. Add burgers and cook until golden brown and cooked through, about 3 minutes per side.

4. Serve on beds of lettuce or on whole-wheat buns with lettuce and tomato.

SERVING SUGGESTION

Enjoy this salad for lunch on some crunchy toast, or for dinner on a fresh bed of greens.

GRAPE & WALNUT CHICKEN SALAD

Prep time: 5 minutes
Container: Nutri Bowl™
Makes: 4 servings

INGREDIENTS

1 celery stalk, cut in quarters

2 cups cooked chicken, cubed, cooled

¼ cup walnuts

½ cup mayonnaise

½ teaspoon salt

¼ teaspoon ground black pepper

¼ teaspoon onion powder

⅓ cup red grapes

DIRECTIONS

1. Place all ingredients into the Nutri Bowl in the order listed.

2. Select Auto-iQ™ BOOST NO Fusion CHOP.

DO NOT BLEND HOT INGREDIENTS.

TACO NIGHT

Prep time: 15 minutes **Cook time:** 6–8 minutes
Container: Nutri Bowl™
Makes: 8 tacos

INGREDIENTS

1/2 medium yellow onion, cut in quarters

1 pound uncooked boneless turkey breast, cut in 2-inch cubes

1 tablespoon canola oil

1 package (1 ounce) low-sodium taco seasoning mix

8 hard taco shells

1 cup shredded lettuce

1/2 cup shredded lowfat cheddar cheese

1/4 cup sliced jalapeño peppers

1/3 cup cilantro

Chipotle Salsa (page 50)

DIRECTIONS

1. Place the onion and turkey into the Nutri Bowl. PULSE until finely ground.

2. Heat the oil in a medium skillet over medium heat. Sauté turkey mixture for 6 to 8 minutes, or until cooked. Add taco seasoning mix and stir to combine.

3. Assemble each taco with cooked turkey, lettuce, cheese, jalapeño, cilantro, and our Best Blender Salsa.

RECIPE SUGGESTION

Customize taco night by using boneless chicken breast, salmon, or shrimp.

CRAB CAKE SLIDERS

Prep time: 15 minutes **Chill time:** 30 minutes **Cook time:** 10 minutes
Container: Nutri Bowl™
Makes: 12 sliders

INGREDIENTS

3 tablespoons light mayonnaise

1 teaspoon Dijon mustard

1 tablespoon lemon juice

1 large egg

2 teaspoons crab seasoning

¼ cup roasted red peppers

¼ cup scallions,
cut into 2-inch pieces

½ cup unseasoned bread crumbs

1 pound jumbo lump crabmeat

1 tablespoon olive oil

DIRECTIONS

1. Place mayonnaise, mustard, lemon juice, egg, crab seasoning, roasted red peppers, and scallions into the Nutri Bowl.

2. Select Auto-iQ™ BOOST YES Fusion CHOP.

3. Transfer mixture to a mixing bowl. Add bread crumbs and crabmeat, folding gently. Form mixture into 12 patties and place in refrigerator for 30 minutes to firm up and hold shape.

4. In a nonstick sauté pan, heat oil over medium-high heat. Sauté crab cakes until browned on both sides and heated through, about 5 minutes per side.

DEVILED BEAN-STUFFED EGGS

Prep time: 10 minutes
Container: Nutri Bowl™
Makes: 24 servings

INGREDIENTS

12 hard-boiled eggs, cut in half lengthwise, yolks removed and reserved

1 can (15 ounces) white beans, rinsed, drained

$\frac{1}{4}$ cup roasted red peppers

2 tablespoons mayonnaise

2 tablespoons sweet pickle relish

1 tablespoon Dijon mustard

1 teaspoon hot sauce

$\frac{1}{2}$ teaspoon paprika, for garnish

DIRECTIONS

1. Place 16 yolk halves, white beans, roasted red peppers, mayonnaise, pickle relish, mustard, and hot sauce into the Nutri Bowl. Select Auto-iQ™ BOOST YES Fusion CHOP.

2. Using a spoon, stuff each egg-white half with bean mixture. Sprinkle with paprika to garnish.

MINI CAULIFLOWER PIZZAS

Prep time: 20 minutes **Cook time:** 40 minutes **Cool time:** 15 minutes
Container: Nutri Bowl™
Makes: 4 mini pizzas

INGREDIENTS

½ head cauliflower,
cut in 1-inch florets

1 ½ cups shredded mozzarella
cheese, divided

⅓ cup shredded
Parmesan cheese

1 large egg

¾ teaspoon Italian seasoning

½ teaspoon salt

¼ teaspoon garlic powder

1 cup pizza sauce

DIRECTIONS

1. Preheat oven to 350°F. Line a baking pan with a silicone baking mat or parchment paper and coat with cooking spray; set aside.

2. Working in batches, place cauliflower into the Nutri Bowl. Select Auto-iQ™ BOOST NO Fusion CHOP until cauliflower is broken down evenly.

3. Add cauliflower to a medium saucepan and cover with water. Cook over medium high heat until cauliflower is tender, about 10 to 12 minutes. Set aside to cool, about 15 minutes. Squeeze out excess liquid with tea towel.

4. In a medium mixing bowl, combine cauliflower, ½ cup mozzarella cheese, Parmesan, egg, Italian seasoning, salt, and garlic powder. Transfer mixture to baking pan and divide into 4 portions. Form circles by spreading and pressing mixture to resemble a crust.

5. Bake 25 minutes. Remove from oven and top with pizza sauce and remaining 1 cup of mozzarella cheese. Bake an additional 5 minutes or until cheese is bubbling.

PIZZA DOUGH

Prep time: 5 minutes **Rest time:** 1 hour
Container: Nutri Bowl™
Makes: 2 (10-inch) pizza doughs

INGREDIENTS

1 packet active dry yeast

1 ½ teaspoons sugar

²/₃ cup warm water

2 cups all-purpose flour

½ teaspoon salt

¼ cup extra-virgin olive oil

DIRECTIONS

1. Combine the yeast, sugar, and warm water in a small bowl and set aside until foamy, about 5 minutes.

2. Position the Dough Blade Assembly in the Nutri Bowl, then add the flour, salt, olive oil, and yeast mixture.

3. Select Auto-iQ™ BOOST YES Fusion DOUGH.

4. Place dough ball into a lightly oiled bowl and cover loosely with plastic wrap. Let rise in a warm place for 1 hour or until doubled in size.

5. Cut dough ball in half. Roll out one half to desired thickness and place on a lightly oiled pan. Repeat with other half or wrap in plastic and store in freezer for up to 2 months.

6. Top with your favorite pizza toppings.

MARGHERITA PIZZA

Prep time: 8 minutes **Cook time:** 15–20 minutes
Container: Nutri Bowl™
Makes: 1 (10-inch) pizza

INGREDIENTS

1 (10-inch) pizza dough
(recipe page 86)

2 vine-ripened tomatoes,
cut in quarters

¼ cup fresh basil leaves

¾ teaspoon ground
black pepper

8 ounces fresh mozzarella
cheese, cut in 1 ½-inch pieces

DIRECTIONS

1. Preheat oven to 400°F. Lightly coat a 10-inch pizza pan with cooking spray.

2. Place prepared pizza dough on top of the pan. Gently and evenly flatten out the dough all the way to the edges; set aside.

3. Place tomatoes, basil, and black pepper into the Nutri Bowl. Select Auto-iQ™ BOOST YES Fusion CHOP. Spoon sauce over dough.

4. Place cheese into the Nutri Bowl. Select START/STOP for 25 seconds. Sprinkle cheese over the sauce.

5. Bake 15 to 20 minutes, or until crust is golden brown.

BROCCOLI TOTS

Prep time: 20 minutes   **Cook time:** 30 minutes
Container: Nutri Bowl™
Makes: 24 tots

INGREDIENTS

2 ½ cups broccoli florets

⅛ medium onion

1 large egg

½ cup shredded cheddar cheese

⅔ cup panko bread crumbs

¼ teaspoon salt

¼ teaspoon ground black pepper

DIRECTIONS

1. Preheat oven to 400°F. Line a baking pan with parchment paper and coat with cooking spray; set aside.

2. In a medium saucepan, bring 1 quart water to a boil. Blanch broccoli for 1 minute. Remove broccoli and cool in ice water. Drain well.

3. Place broccoli and onion into the Nutri Bowl. Select Auto-iQ™ BOOST NO Fusion CHOP.

4. Transfer mixture into a medium mixing bowl. Add egg, cheese, bread crumbs, salt, and pepper and mix thoroughly.

5. Shape mixture into 24 cylinders about ¾ inch wide by 1 inch long. Place on prepared baking pan and bake 25 minutes, or until tots are crispy, gently flipping halfway through.

DO NOT BLEND HOT INGREDIENTS.

CHEESE DROP BISCUITS

Prep time: 15 minutes **Cook time:** 12 minutes
Container: Nutri Bowl™
Makes: 9 servings

INGREDIENTS

1 1/3 cups all-purpose flour

2 teaspoons baking powder

2 teaspoons sugar

1/4 teaspoon salt

1/8 teaspoon baking soda

6 tablespoons unsalted butter, melted

2/3 cup milk

2/3 cup shredded cheddar cheese

DIRECTIONS

1. Preheat oven to 450°F. Line a baking sheet with parchment paper; set aside.

2. In a medium bowl, whisk together flour, baking powder, sugar, salt, and baking soda until evenly combined.

3. Position the Dough Blade Assembly in the Nutri Bowl, then add the dry-ingredient mixture, melted butter, and milk.

4. Select Auto-iQ™ BOOST YES Fusion DOUGH. Mixture will be wet.

5. Place dough into a mixing bowl. Add cheese and lightly mix until incorporated.

6. Drop dough 2 tablespoons at a time onto the prepared baking pan and bake 12 minutes or until edges of biscuits are golden brown.

VEGGIE BURGERS

Prep time: 15 minutes **Cook time:** 15 minutes
Container: Nutri Bowl™
Makes: 4 (6-ounce) burgers

INGREDIENTS

¼ medium onion

½ medium carrot, peeled,
cut in 1-inch pieces

1 can (15 ounces) black beans,
rinsed, drained, divided

½ cup cooked quinoa

1 large egg

½ cup bread crumbs

1 teaspoon salt

1 teaspoon ground black pepper

½ teaspoon ground cumin

½ teaspoon smoked paprika

1 tablespoon canola oil

DIRECTIONS

1. Place onion and carrot into the Nutri Bowl. Select Auto-iQ™ BOOST NO Fusion CHOP. Add ½ the black beans to Nutri Bowl. Select Auto-iQ BOOST YES Fusion CHOP.

2. Transfer onion mixture to a medium mixing bowl. Add remaining black beans, quinoa, egg, bread crumbs, salt, pepper, cumin, and paprika. Stir to combine.

3. Divide mixture evenly and shape into 4 patties. Add canola oil to a large sauté pan over medium-high heat. When oil is hot, add patties. Cook 8 minutes, or until heated through, flipping halfway through cooking.

4. Serve over a salad or on a toasted bun.

**SERVING
SUGGESTION**

Serve with honey
mustard or your
favorite dipping sauce.

PRETZEL-COATED CHICKEN FINGERS

Prep time: 15 minutes **Cook time:** 18 minutes
Container: Nutri Bowl™
Makes: 4 servings

INGREDIENTS

2 cups mini pretzels

1 large egg

1 tablespoon water

¼ cup all-purpose flour

½ teaspoon salt

½ teaspoon ground black pepper

1 pound uncooked boneless chicken tenderloins

DIRECTIONS

1. Preheat oven to 350°F. Lightly coat a baking pan with cooking spray; set aside.

2. Place pretzels into the Nutri Bowl. Select START/STOP for 15 seconds. Transfer mixture to a small mixing bowl.

3. In a separate mixing bowl, whisk egg and 1 tablespoon water. In another bowl, place flour, salt, and pepper.

4. Coat each chicken tenderloin in flour, removing any excess, then in egg wash, and finally in pretzel mixture.

5. Place coated chicken tenderloins on baking pan and lightly coat both sides with cooking spray. Bake for 18 minutes or until cooked through.

LATIN EMPANADAS

Prep time: 5 minutes **Cook time:** 1 hour
Container: 24-ounce Tritan™ Nutri Ninja® Cup
Makes: 6 servings

INGREDIENTS

1 cup canned coconut milk

½ cup tapioca flour

½ cup brown rice flour

1 tablespoon canola oil

⅓ pound (6 ounces)
lean ground beef

¼ medium onion, chopped

¼ cup tomato sauce

⅓ cup sliced Spanish olives
with pimentos

1 teaspoon ground cumin

½ teaspoon dried oregano

½ teaspoon salt

½ teaspoon ground black pepper

1 large egg white

1 tablespoon water

DIRECTIONS

1. Preheat oven to 325°F. Line a baking pan with parchment paper and coat with cooking spray; set aside.

2. Place coconut milk, tapioca flour, and brown rice flour into the 24-ounce Tritan Nutri Ninja Cup.

3. Select START/STOP until combined, about 15 seconds.

4. Remove blades from cup after blending.

5. Heat a nonstick sauté pan over medium heat. Pour ¼ cup batter into pan. Cook batter for 2 minutes. Flip and cook an additional 2 minutes. Remove empanada shell and repeat with remaining batter.

6. Add oil to a sauté pan over medium heat. Allow oil to heat for 2 minutes. Add ground beef and cook until browned, breaking up meat with a spoon, about 5 minutes. Add onions and cook until softened, about 4 minutes. Add tomato sauce, olives, cumin, oregano, salt, and pepper. Simmer until mixture thickens, about 5 minutes. Remove from heat and cool.

7. Divide meat mixture equally into the middle of each empanada shell. In a small bowl, combine egg white with 1 tablespoon water. Brush inner edges of empanadas with egg wash, then fold in half and pinch dough closed.

8. Place empanadas on the prepared baking pan and bake 35 minutes or until crispy and golden brown. Flip empanadas halfway through baking.

FALAFEL

Prep time: 5 minutes **Rest time:** 1 hour **Cook time:** 10 minutes
Container: Nutri Bowl™
Makes: 9 servings

INGREDIENTS

1 can (15 ounces)
garbanzo beans, drained

¼ medium onion

4 cloves garlic, peeled

3 tablespoons fresh
parsley leaves

½ teaspoon crushed red pepper

1 teaspoon ground cumin

1 teaspoon salt

1 teaspoon baking powder

¼ cup all-purpose flour

2 cups canola oil, for frying

DIRECTIONS

1. Place garbanzo beans, onion, garlic, and parsley into the Nutri Bowl. Select Auto-iQ™ BOOST NO Fusion MIX.

2. Place garbanzo mixture, crushed red pepper, cumin, salt, baking powder, and flour into a medium mixing bowl, and stir to combine. Cover and refrigerate 1 hour.

3. Form mixture into 2-inch round balls. Add oil to a large sauté pan over medium high heat. Once oil is hot, carefully add falafel. Cook for 4 minutes or until golden brown on all sides. Drain on paper towels.

PEAR, GRUYÈRE & ROSEMARY FLATBREAD

Prep time: 15 minutes **Rise time:** 1 hour **Cook time:** 10-15 minutes
Container: Nutri Bowl™
Makes: 4–6 servings

INGREDIENTS

WHOLE-WHEAT FLATBREAD

1 packet (¼ ounce)
dry active yeast

1 teaspoon salt

1 tablespoon sugar

⅔ cup warm water (110°F–115°F)

¼ cup extra-virgin olive oil

1 cup unbleached,
all-purpose flour

1 ¼ cups whole-wheat flour

Cornmeal, for dusting

TOPPINGS

½ cup shredded Gruyère or
Swiss cheese

1 large pear, thinly sliced

2 tablespoons fresh rosemary,
stems removed, minced

DIRECTIONS

1. Preheat oven to 450°F.

2. Position the Dough Blade Assembly in the Nutri Bowl,
   then add yeast, salt, sugar, and water; PULSE to combine.

3. Add oil and flours, and select Auto-iQ™ BOOST YES Fusion
   DOUGH until a loose ball forms. Transfer dough to a lightly
   oiled bowl and cover. Let rise for 1 hour.

4. Sprinkle a 10x15-inch baking sheet with cornmeal and roll
   out or press the dough into a thin round. Lay pear slices on
   top and sprinkle evenly with shredded cheese.

5. Bake 10 to 15 minutes, or until cheese has melted and crust
   is golden brown. Garnish with fresh rosemary.

RECIPE SUGGESTION

Try with any of your favorite toppings such as pepperoni, mozzarella, arugula, or grilled portobello mushrooms.

VEGETARIAN EGG ROLLS

Prep time: 25 minutes **Cook time:** 21 minutes
Container: Nutri Bowl™
Makes: 6 servings

INGREDIENTS

1 ³/₄ cups green cabbage,
cut in 1-inch pieces

1 medium carrot, peeled,
cut in 1-inch pieces

1 stalk celery,
cut in 1-inch pieces

2 green onions,
cut in 1-inch pieces

1 tablespoon canola oil

3 tablespoons soy sauce

1 teaspoon cornstarch

¹/₂ teaspoon sesame oil

¹/₂ teaspoon ground black pepper

¹/₄ teaspoon ground ginger

6 egg roll wrappers

DIRECTIONS

1. Preheat oven to 375°F. Line a baking sheet with parchment paper; set aside.

2. Place cabbage, carrot, celery, and green onions into the Nutri Bowl. Select Auto-iQ™ BOOST YES Fusion CHOP.

3. Add oil to a medium sauté pan over medium-high heat. Once oil is hot, add vegetable mixture. Cook for 4 minutes, stirring occasionally, until vegetables start to wilt.

4. In a small bowl, mix soy sauce with cornstarch. Add mixture to pan with vegetables and cook for 1 minute, or until sauce thickens. Remove from heat and let cool.

5. In a small mixing bowl, combine cooled vegetables, sesame oil, pepper, and ginger. Place 2 tablespoons of mixture in center of each egg roll wrapper. Moisten edges with water. Fold 2 sides over, to look like an envelope, then roll forward to seal.

6. Coat egg rolls with cooking spray. Place on prepared baking sheet and bake 16 minutes, or until egg rolls are crispy and light brown. Gently flip rolls halfway through cooking.

GARLIC KNOTS

Prep time: 10 minutes **Rest time:** 1 ½ hours **Cook time:** 15 minutes
Container: Nutri Bowl™
Makes: 6 knots

INGREDIENTS

1 cup bread flour

1 ⅛ teaspoon active dry yeast

1 ½ teaspoons sugar

½ teaspoon salt

¼ teaspoon garlic powder

1 tablespoon roasted garlic, cooled, chopped

⅓ cup plus 1 tablespoon warm water (110°F–115°F)

2 tablespoons unsalted butter, melted

DIRECTIONS

1. Position the Dough Blade Assembly in the Nutri Bowl, then then add all ingredients in the order listed.

2. Select Auto-iQ™ BOOST YES Fusion DOUGH.

3. Place dough ball into a lightly oiled bowl, cover loosely with plastic wrap, and let rise in a warm place for 1 ½ hours or until double in size.

4. Preheat oven to 400°F. Line a baking sheet with parchment paper; set aside.

5. Divide dough into 6 equal portions and roll them into 7-inch long ropes, about ½-inch thick. Tie each into a knot, tucking in the ends. Place onto the prepared baking sheet and bake 15 minutes or until golden brown.

DO NOT BLEND HOT INGREDIENTS.

RECIPE SUGGESTION

Add cooked chicken, shrimp, or tofu for a quick one-pot meal.

CAULIFLOWER FRIED RICE

Prep time: 10 minutes **Cook time:** 10 minutes
Container: Nutri Bowl™
Makes: 2 cups

INGREDIENTS

3 cups cauliflower

1 medium carrot, peeled, cut in 1-inch pieces

1-inch piece fresh ginger, peeled

2 tablespoons sesame oil

2 green onions, chopped

½ cup peas

2 tablespoons soy sauce

¼ teaspoon black pepper

DIRECTIONS

1. Place cauliflower into the Nutri Bowl. Select Auto-iQ™ BOOST NO Fusion CHOP.

2. Place carrot and ginger into the Nutri Bowl. Select Auto-iQ BOOST YES Fusion CHOP.

3. Add sesame oil to a medium sauté pan over medium-high heat. Allow pan to heat for 1 minute, then add cauliflower and carrot mixture. Cook for 5 minutes or until cauliflower is tender, stirring occasionally. Add green onions, peas, soy sauce, and pepper. Cook for 2 minutes or until heated through.

DARK CHOCOLATE CHIP MOUSSE

Prep time: 5 minutes **Chill time:** 20 minutes
Container: Nutri Bowl™
Makes: 3 cups (4–6 servings)

INGREDIENTS

1 ½ cups heavy
whipping cream, cold

¼ cup dark chocolate syrup

⅓ cup semisweet chocolate chips

DIRECTIONS

1. Place all ingredients into the Nutri Bowl in the order listed.

2. Select Auto-iQ™ BOOST YES Fusion MIX.

3. Place mousse in an airtight container and freeze for 20 minutes, or until chilled and firm.

**SERVING
SUGGESTION**

Enjoy atop a bowl of
fresh berries for a quick
and impressive dessert.

FROZEN CAMPFIRE

Prep time: 5 minutes
Container: 24-ounce Tritan™ Nutri Ninja® Cup
Makes: 2 (8-ounce) servings

INGREDIENTS

1 cup 2% milk

$^1/_2$ cup marshmallow cream

$^3/_4$ cup graham cracker crumbs

1 $^1/_2$ cups chocolate frozen yogurt

DIRECTIONS

1. Place all ingredients into the 24-ounce Tritan Nutri Ninja Cup in the order listed.

2. Select Auto-iQ™ BOOST NO SMOOTHIE.

3. Remove blades from cup after blending.

CRUSHED PEPPERMINT FROZEN FRAPPE

Prep time: 5 minutes
Container: 24-ounce Tritan™ Nutri Ninja® Cup
Makes: 2 (10-ounce) servings

INGREDIENTS

¹/₂ cup almond milk

2 cups lowfat vanilla
frozen yogurt

10 peppermint candies

Peppermint sticks, for garnish

DIRECTIONS

1. Place all ingredients into the 24-ounce Tritan Nutri Ninja Cup in the order listed.

2. Select START/STOP until smooth.

3. Remove blades from cup after blending.

4. Serve in small glasses garnished with peppermint sticks.

NO-BAKE MINI CHEESECAKES

Prep time: 25 minutes **Chill time:** 4 hours
Container: Nutri Bowl™
Makes: 12 servings

INGREDIENTS

2 ½ cups honey graham crackers, chopped

¼ cup light brown sugar

¼ cup (4 tablespoons) unsalted butter, melted

1 package (8 ounces) cream cheese, softened

¼ cup sugar

1 teaspoon lemon juice

½ teaspoon vanilla extract

1 tub (8 ounces) whipped topping, thawed

DIRECTIONS

1. Line a standard 12-cup muffin tin with paper or aluminum liners. Lightly coat the inside of the liners with cooking spray; set aside.

2. Place graham crackers, brown sugar, and butter into the Nutri Bowl.

3. Select Auto iQ™ BOOST YES Fusion MIX.

4. Divide mixture evenly in the prepared muffin tin. Press on mixture until firmly packed; set aside.

5. Place cream cheese, sugar, lemon juice, and vanilla into the Nutri Bowl.

6. Select Auto-iQ BOOST NO Fusion MIX. Remove lid and scrape down sides of bowl. Select START/STOP for 15 seconds or until mixture is creamy and well combined.

7. Spoon cream cheese mixture into a bowl and gently fold in whipped topping until evenly incorporated.

8. Spoon cheesecake mixture into prepared muffin tins and spread to level it. Refrigerate at least 4 hours or overnight.

DULCE DE LECHE BARS

Prep time: 15 minutes   **Cook time:** 10 minutes   **Rest time:** 6 hours
Container: Nutri Bowl™
Makes: 16 servings

INGREDIENTS

2 cups roughly crushed saltine crackers, divided

¼ cup sugar

6 tablespoons unsalted butter, melted

1 can (13.4 ounces) dulce de leche

DIRECTIONS

1. Preheat oven to 325°F. Lightly coat an 8x8-inch baking pan with cooking spray. Line with parchment paper and lightly coat with cooking spray again; set aside.

2. Place 1 ½ cups saltine crackers and sugar into the Nutri Bowl. Select Auto-iQ™ BOOST YES Fusion CHOP.

3. Add melted butter and select Auto-iQ BOOST YES Fusion CHOP.

4. Spoon mixture into the prepared baking pan and press into bottom of pan until evenly spread. Bake for 10 minutes or until lightly browned.

5. Remove from oven and immediately dollop the dulce de leche on top. Gently spread over the crust until completely covered. Sprinkle the remaining ½ cup saltine crackers on top.

6. Let stand at room temperature for at least 6 hours, or overnight.

PREP SUGGESTION

These bars need the time to rest to set to the proper texture—it's worth the wait.

LEMON BARS

Prep time: 20 minutes **Cook time:** 35–40 minutes
Container: Nutri Bowl™
Makes: 12 servings

INGREDIENTS

2 sticks (1 cup) unsalted butter, softened

2 cups sugar, divided

2 1/3 cups all-purpose flour, divided

4 large eggs

2/3 cup freshly squeezed lemon juice

Confectioners' sugar, for garnish

DIRECTIONS

1. Preheat oven to 350°F.

2. Position the Dough Blade Assembly in the Nutri Bowl, then add the butter, 1/2 cup sugar, and 2 cups flour. Select Auto-iQ™ BOOST YES Fusion CHOP adding additional pulses until dough just comes together.

3. Press dough into the bottom of an ungreased 9x13-inch baking dish. Bake 15 minutes, or until firm and golden in color. Cool for 10 minutes.

4. Place the remaining 1 1/2 cups sugar, remaining 1/3 cup flour, eggs, and lemon juice into the Nutri Bowl. Select START/STOP; blend until smooth and sugar is dissolved.

5. Pour lemon mixture over the par-baked crust. Bake 20 to 25 minutes. Lemon bars will be soft after baking but will firm as they cool.

6. Once completely cooled, dust with confectioners' sugar.

BROWNIE CUPS

Prep time: 15 minutes **Cook time:** 25 minutes
Container: Nutri Bowl™
Makes: 9 brownie cups

INGREDIENTS

²/₃ cup sugar

¹/₃ cup all-purpose flour

¹/₈ teaspoon baking powder

¹/₄ cup unsweetened
cocoa powder

¹/₄ teaspoon salt

¹/₄ teaspoon instant
espresso granules

2 tablespoons unsalted butter,
melted

2 tablespoons canola oil

1 large egg, lightly beaten

¹/₂ teaspoon vanilla extract

³/₄ cup semi-sweet
chocolate chips

DIRECTIONS

1. Preheat oven to 375°F. Line a 12-cup muffin tin with paper or aluminum liners. Lightly coat the inside of the liners with cooking spray; set aside.

2. Position the Dough Blade Assembly in the Nutri Bowl; then add the sugar, flour, baking powder, cocoa powder, salt, and instant espresso. Select Auto-iQ™ BOOST NO Fusion CHOP.

3. Add the dry-ingredient mixture, butter, oil, egg, and vanilla to the Nutri Bowl. Select Auto-iQ BOOST YES Fusion DOUGH.

4. Remove lid and carefully scrape down sides of bowl. Add chocolate chips and select START/STOP for 10 seconds.

5. Divide mixture evenly into the prepared muffin tins. Bake 25 minutes, or until just set in the middle.

SERVING SUGGESTION

Serve this delicious dessert in waffle-cone bowls for added fun.

BANANA SPLIT FROZEN DESSERT

Prep time: 4 minutes
Container: Nutri Bowl™
Makes: 1 ½ cups (3 servings)

INGREDIENTS

½ small frozen ripe banana, cut in quarters

1 ¼ cups frozen strawberries

¼ cup walnut halves

1 tablespoon honey

½ cup light cream

Whipped cream, for garnish

Sprinkles, for garnish

Cherries, for garnish

DIRECTIONS

1. Place all ingredients into the Nutri Bowl in the order listed.

2. Select Auto-iQ™ BOOST YES Fusion MIX.

3. Serve with whipped cream, sprinkles, and a cherry, or your desired toppings.

CHOCOLATE RASPBERRY TART

Prep time: 30 minutes   **Cook time:** 12 minutes   **Rest time:** 15 minutes
Container: Nutri Bowl™
Makes: 8 servings

INGREDIENTS

2 cups roughly crushed chocolate sandwich cookies

¼ cup whole almonds

2 tablespoons sugar

¼ cup (4 tablespoons) unsalted butter, melted, divided

1 ½ cups semisweet chocolate chips, melted

2 cups fresh raspberries

DIRECTIONS

1. Preheat oven to 350°F. Lightly coat an 8-inch tart pan with cooking spray; set aside.

2. Place cookies, almonds, and sugar into the Nutri Bowl.

3. Select Auto-iQ™ BOOST YES Fusion CHOP until mixture is ground. Add melted butter, then select Auto-iQ BOOST YES Fusion CHOP until combined.

4. Spoon mixture into the prepared baking pan and press on bottom and sides of pan until evenly spread. Bake 10 to 12 minutes. Remove from oven and let cool for 15 minutes.

5. Pour melted chocolate over the crust and spread to cover completely. Place raspberries over the melted chocolate and serve.

RECIPE SUGGESTION

For a variation, try using white chocolate chips, with vanilla sandwich cookies in the crust.

NO-BAKE VEGAN COOKIE DOUGH

Prep time: 10 minutes
Container: Nutri Bowl™
Makes: 15 cookies

INGREDIENTS

³/₄ cup unsalted cashews

³/₄ cup old-fashioned rolled oats

³/₄ teaspoon salt

2 tablespoons sugar

³/₄ teaspoon vanilla extract

¼ cup maple syrup

¼ cup vegan mini
dark chocolate chips

DIRECTIONS

1. Place cashews and oats into the Nutri Bowl. Select Auto-iQ™ BOOST YES Fusion CHOP. Mixture will be crumbly.

2. Add salt, sugar, vanilla, and maple syrup to the Nutri Bowl. Select Auto-iQ BOOST NO Fusion DOUGH. Dough will be slightly sticky.

3. Place the chocolate chips into the Nutri Bowl. Select Auto-iQ BOOST NO Fusion CHOP.

4. Roll dough into 1-tablespoon-size balls. Place in an airtight container (other than the Nutri Bowl) and store in the freezer up to 1 month.

CINNAMON SUGAR CHEESECAKE BARS

Prep time: 15 minutes **Cook time:** 35 minutes **Chill time:** 3 hours
Container: Nutri Bowl™
Makes: 8–10 servings

INGREDIENTS

2 ½ cups roughly crushed cinnamon graham crackers

¼ cup dark brown sugar

¼ teaspoon ground cinnamon

¼ cup (4 tablespoons) unsalted butter, melted

1 package (8 ounces) cream cheese, softened

¼ cup sugar

¾ teaspoon vanilla extract

1 large egg, lightly beaten

DIRECTIONS

1. Preheat oven to 350°F. Lightly coat an 8x8-inch baking pan with cooking spray; set aside.

2. Place graham crackers, brown sugar, and cinnamon into the Nutri Bowl.

3. Select Auto-iQ™ BOOST NO Fusion DOUGH.

4. Add melted butter, select Auto-iQ BOOST NO Fusion DOUGH.

5. Spoon mixture into the prepared baking pan and press into bottom of pan until evenly spread. Bake 10 minutes or until lightly browned.

6. Place cream cheese, sugar, vanilla, and egg into the Nutri Bowl.

7. Select START/STOP and blend for 20 seconds or until mixture is creamy and well combined.

8. Pour batter over warm crust and spread until even. Bake 25 minutes or until filling is set.

9. Remove from oven and place on a cooling rack. Let cool completely. Refrigerate at least 3 hours or overnight before serving.

SALTED CARAMEL CHIP COOKIES

Prep time: 20 minutes **Cook time:** 8–10 minutes
Container: Nutri Bowl™
Makes: 15 cookies

INGREDIENTS

¼ cup unsalted butter, softened

½ teaspoon vanilla extract

¼ cup light brown sugar, firmly packed

⅛ cup white sugar

½ teaspoon salt

1 cup all-purpose flour

¼ teaspoon baking soda

1 extra large egg, lightly beaten

⅔ cup caramel or toffee bits

DIRECTIONS

1. Preheat oven to 350°F. Line a baking sheet with parchment paper; set aside.

2. Position the Dough Blade Assembly in the Nutri Bowl, then add all ingredients, except caramel or toffee bits, in the order listed.

3. Select Auto-iQ™ BOOST YES Fusion DOUGH.

4. Add caramel or toffee bits to the Nutri Bowl and select Auto-iQ BOOST NO Fusion CHOP. Then carefully scrape down sides of bowl with spatula.

5. Scoop dough by the tablespoonful onto prepared baking sheet 2 inches apart. Bake 8 to 10 minutes, or until light golden brown.

BLUEBERRY LEMON SORBET

Prep time: 4 minutes **Chill time:** 20 minutes
Container: Nutri Bowl™
Makes: 2 cups (4 servings)

INGREDIENTS

1 ³/₄ cups frozen blueberries

3 mint leaves

²/₃ cup lemonade

DIRECTIONS

1. Place all ingredients into the Nutri Bowl in the order listed.

2. Select Auto-iQ™ BOOST YES Fusion MIX.

3. Place sorbet in an airtight container in the freezer for 20 minutes, or until chilled and firm.

PEACH GINGERSNAP TART

Prep time: 15 minutes **Cook time:** 20–25 minutes
Container: Nutri Bowl™
Makes: 8 servings

INGREDIENTS

2 cups gingersnaps, roughly crushed

¼ cup light brown sugar

5 tablespoons unsalted butter, melted, divided

3 cups frozen sliced peaches, thawed

⅓ cup sugar

½ teaspoon almond extract

DIRECTIONS

1. Preheat oven to 350°F. Lightly coat an 8-inch tart pan with cooking spray; set aside.

2. Place gingersnaps and brown sugar into the Nutri Bowl. Select Auto-iQ™ BOOST YES Fusion CHOP.

3. Add 3 tablespoons melted butter and select Auto-iQ BOOST YES Fusion CHOP.

4. Spoon mixture into the prepared baking pan and press into bottom and sides of pan until evenly spread. Bake 15 minutes. Remove from oven and let cool completely.

5. In a mixing bowl, toss the peaches, sugar, and almond extract. Melt 2 tablespoons butter in a medium sauté pan. Add peach mixture and cook, over medium heat, until peaches are tender and caramelized. Let cool completely.

6. Spoon peach mixture into crust.

BLUEBERRY CRUMBLE PIE

Prep time: 40 minutes **Chill time:** 1 hour 30 minutes **Cook time:** 1 hour 35 minutes
Container: Nutri Bowl™
Makes: 8 servings

INGREDIENTS

2 ⅛ cups all-purpose flour, divided

¾ teaspoon salt, divided

9 tablespoons cold unsalted butter, cut in ½-inch cubes, divided

3 tablespoons cold shortening, cut in ½-inch cubes

¼-⅓ cup ice-cold water

½ cup granulated sugar

Zest of 2 lemons

3 ½ cups blueberries

½ cup light brown sugar, packed

½ cup old fashioned rolled oats

¼ teaspoon salt

½ teaspoon ground cinnamon

DIRECTIONS

1. Place 1 ⅓ cups flour and ½ teaspoon salt into the Nutri Bowl. Select Auto-iQ™ BOOST NO Fusion CHOP.

2. Add 3 tablespoons butter and 3 tablespoons shortening. Select Auto-iQ BOOST YES Fusion DOUGH. While machine is running, drizzle in cold water until dough just starts to come together.

3. Turn the dough out onto a large piece of plastic wrap and press it into a 1-inch thick disk. Wrap tightly in the plastic wrap and refrigerate for 1 hour.

4. Place dough onto a lightly floured surface and roll into a 12-inch round. Place dough in center of a 9-inch pie plate. Fold the overhang under itself and crimp the edges. Refrigerate for 30 minutes.

5. Preheat oven to 350°F. Lightly pierce the bottom and sides of the crust with a fork, then line with parchment paper and fill with pie weights. Bake 20 minutes, then remove parchment paper and pie weights and continue baking until lightly golden, about 15 minutes. Transfer to a rack and let cool completely. Increase oven temperature to 375°F.

6. In a large bowl, gently toss ⅓ cup flour, granulated sugar, lemon zest, and blueberries. Pour into the pie crust.

7. Position the Dough Blade Assembly in the Nutri Bowl, then add ½ cup flour, 6 tablespoons butter, brown sugar, oats, ¼ teaspoon salt, and cinnamon.

8. Select Auto-iQ BOOST YES Fusion CHOP. Mixture will be crumbly. Sprinkle dough mixture over blueberry filling.

9. Bake 1 hour or until golden brown. Let cool completely.

RECIPE SUGGESTION

For the flakiest pie dough, put the butter and shortening cubes in the freezer for 20 minutes just before using.

INDEX

TAKEOUT AT HOME

DESSERTS & FROZEN TREATS